Ride It Out On This Side
Or Wait It Out
On The Other Side

VESTER DOCK

Ride It Out On This Side
Or Wait It Out On The Other Side

Copyright © 2018 by Vester Dock

All rights reserved. No part of this book may be reproduced or transmitted in any form or by any means without written permission of the author.

ISBN 978-0-9822796-7-0

Cover Design: Donna Osborn Clark at CreationsByDonna@gmail.com

Layout and Interior Design: Creative Unity Productions

Editing: Inkaissance at inkaissance@gmail.com

Scriptures from the King James Version of the *Holy Bible*

Published by: Dove Gray Publishing
DoveGrayPub@gmail.com

Manufactured in the United States of America

First Edition

This book written in memory of Gail

Dedicated to my lovely wife Emma and kids; and my extended family at New Hope Baptist Church, 28 First Street, Freehold, New Jersey 07728.

Table of Contents

Section One 1

Section Two 17

Section Three 31

Resources 49

Notes & Reflections 57

Section One

Advise Concerning Life and Death

There are various reasons that I am writing this book. Mainly because in 2014 and 2015 suicidal death seemed overwhelming which caused me to believe there is something far beyond mental and physical pressure that is involved with it. Donald Trump and Military Times News were quoted as saying that an average of 20 military veterans committed suicidal death daily. My heart ached as my mind wondered if we over looking something that the person themselves were not aware of. By me knowing a little about God and being much acquainted with the demonic spirit Satan as well, I did not know how I may help but as I watched Diane Sawyer, an American television journalist on ABC news nightly flagship program, she asked if anyone had something that they though may help people who were thinking of committing suicide. Whether we are believers or unbelievers, this evil spirit is able to overpower us without the power of God's spirit, which I believe lives within us.

Galatians 5:17

[17] For the flesh lusteth against the Spirit, and the Spirit against the flesh: and these are contrary the one to the other: so that ye cannot do the things that ye would.

So, if one is aware that there may be forces within, maybe you can understand that you are being persuaded to commit suicidal death and it's not by choice. So if we say it's our life and our choice then the result of suicidal death, may not be our choice. There may be a penalty, for one of us shall give account of himself to God.

Ride It Out On This Side Or Wait It Out On The Other Side

Romans 14:7-8

[7] For none of us liveth to himself, and no man dieth to himself.
[8] For whether we live, we live unto the Lord; and whether we die, we die unto the Lord: whether we live therefore, or die, we are the Lord's.

With that being said, suicidal death is a way to avoid struggle, disappointment, worries, aggravation and trouble in life. We do not know what awaits us after death. I do not know what awaits us after death. I do not know whether or not if suicidal death carries a penalty or if more trouble awaits us on the other side, than the struggles we already face on this side. All I am saying is this… Whatsoever you struggle with on this side, "ride" it out on this side or wait it out on the other side. Whether we die at the hand of God or by the hands of suicide…

Vester Dock

2 Corinthians 5:10

¹⁰ For we must all appear before the judgment seat of Christ; that every one may receive the things done in his body, according to that he hath done, whether it be good or bad.

My friends, sisters and brothers please believe me. I am not trying to change anyone's religious beliefs. I am just trying to give you hope when it seems that you may be in a hopeless situation that may have you wanting to commit suicide. Whether we believe in God or His words, suicidal death will not change God or his word. Nor will it make things better. All I want you to know is that God gave us this life. I am saying that our chances of overcoming our dilemmas are better if we are alive. At the rate of suicidal death over the last two and a half years, I won't believe it's all physical or mental. Many medicines that are sold in stores state that one side effect may be suicidal thoughts.

Now we ask ourselves, "How can we know the difference? Maybe we should try to recall our actions and think before taking the medicine and about our behavior after taking the medicine. Maybe it would be safe to say that the medicine may ease our behavior for a while, "but" this spirit is very, very persistent. Once the mouth speaks suicide this spirit knows how the mind is thinking. This spirit knows the scripture better than most of us.

Matthew 12:34

³⁴ O generation of vipers, how can ye, being evil, speak good things? for out of the abundance of the heart the mouth speaketh.

Proverbs 23:7

⁷ For as he thinketh in his heart, so is he: Eat and drink, saith he to thee;
but his heart is not with thee.

The mind can easily twist the truth and irrationalize the misbehavior and justify it. If we lust to do something this spirit can help find ways to persuade and justify ourselves in doing it. My friend's, there are those who may need medicine "but" I don't believe medicine is the answer to all neither physical nor mental illness... The scripture tells us:

1 John 4:1-3

¹ Beloved, believe not every spirit, but try the spirits whether they are of God: because many false prophets are gone out into the world.
² Hereby know ye the Spirit of God: Every spirit that confesseth that Jesus Christ is come in the flesh is of God: ³ And every spirit that confesseth not that Jesus Christ is come in the flesh is not of God: and this is that spirit of antichrist, whereof ye have heard that it should come; and even now already is it in the world.

I know many preachers, teachers and believers do not talk much about this evil spirit on television and not in all churches either. But, to me if we don't preach or teach about this evil spirit then we are not preaching the entire bible. In many scriptures Jesus talks and teaches about Satan, also known as the devil.

Matthew 4:1

¹ Then was Jesus led up of the Spirit into the wilderness to be tempted of the devil.

Luke 10:18

¹⁸ And he said unto them, I beheld Satan as lightning fall from heaven.

I truly believe we should be aware of another spirit in this world other than the spirit of God… One who can influence and destroy us...

1 Peter 5:8

⁸ Be sober, be vigilant; because your adversary the devil, as a roaring lion, walketh about, seeking whom he may devour:

Satan is seeking whom he may devour and destroy. My hope and prayer is that some these people who are certified and qualified and have the authority to meet with military veterans would take this book along with them to their training and become one with the wounded veterans. I pray they would try to think as they think and look beyond what the eyes see and what the mind may think.

1 Corinthians 9:22

²² To the weak became I as weak, that I might gain the weak: I am made all things to all men, that I might by all means save some.

If we are going to help these veterans from thinking about committing suicide and putting their struggle to rest then we have to think from their view. Their daily dilemma reminds them of warfare and combat, such as Iraq and Afghanistan. I am saying that we must try to think the way he or she is thinking first. Then we must look at their physical dilemma and let them know that we are feeling their pain.

Ride It Out On This Side Or Wait It Out On The Other Side

I believe if they could feel your heart through the words spoken from your mouth, it's like preaching to a congregation. I have learned that the congregation hears the words coming from my mouth, but need to feel the love I have for their soul and my sincere concern for the dilemma's they are struggling with. When your daily struggles make you feel like a failure, nothing can crush a man's spirit like failure. Nothing can push a person to their wits end like failure and also when you begin to feel those whom you love have failed you. You feel more like a failure and then the mind becomes flooded with aggravation, frustration and disappointment. This evil spirit knows that these are enemies to the mind. This is one of the ways that evil spirits influences our minds. He sees our daily struggle and when he sees a sign of weakness his first attack is at our mind. He knoweth that the mind is the tool we think and reason with. To those of you who may be involved in trying to help veterans from committing suicide, if I may, I suggest that you would take a few former soldiers who serviced in similar situations, along with trained staff, so they can be with people who can not only relate to them, but also have the skill set to help them with their struggles in relation to suicidal thoughts. The soldier who fought in the war but survived without any handicap can relate to what the current soldier mind state is. Who better to help than the one saw it first hand? One who lost an arm, leg, and eye or had a bomb paralyze him/her without a doubt is a great person for the task. Their hands on experience show the service we give to try to heal them, by any means necessary.

I know as the government they know that soldiers fight in wars over seas but should not have to come back home to have to fight a war of homelessness, hunger and depression. These factors all can lead to suicidal thoughts. I believe in the minds of these veterans they begin to believe that they are failures because the government failed them. If these veterans are struggling to maintain to support their families because of the high cost of living, then yes, the government had failed them and their families. These are things that can cause a man in his right mind, who's working daily and still struggling to survive, to entertain suicidal thoughts. Depressive thoughts begin to the cloud the mind and one result is changed thinking and behavior.

What I need the government and any of us who are trying to help these soldiers understand is this… The physical war they experienced never left their minds mentally. At times they still think that we are fighting that war. So the mind can cause the heart to cry out and our actions show signs of weakness. That's when evil spirits make their presence known by penetrating our heart.

Proverbs 23:7

⁷ For as he thinketh in his heart, so is he: Eat and drink, saith he to thee; but his heart is not with thee.

Ephesians 2:2

² Wherein in time past ye walked according to the course of this world, according to the prince of the power of the air, the spirit that now worketh in the children of disobedience:

The devil is the prince and power of the air. Once we speak our feelings from the mouth or express them by phone I believe there are fifty trillion air waves that go through the air. Every three to five seconds per-day, by some electronic device, we are exposed to the enemy of this evil spirit.

Matthew 26:41

⁴¹ Watch and pray, that ye enter not into temptation: the spirit indeed is willing, but the flesh is weak.

Galatians 5:17

17 For the flesh lusteth against the Spirit, and the Spirit against the flesh: and these are contrary the one to the other: so that ye cannot do the things that ye would.

I put it this way; the enemy knowneth that we have become a silver war within ourselves.

Now that evil spirit starts making suggestions, trying to persuade, entice and influence us. We have nothing left to hold on to or no one to turn to. If we listen to him we may attempt to commit suicide. I want to warn all of us that this evil is not what Hollywood has portrayed him to be.

Ephesians 6:12

12 For we wrestle not against flesh and blood, but against principalities, against powers, against the rulers of the darkness of this world, against spiritual wickedness in high places.

1 Corinthians 8:2

2 And if any man think that he knoweth any thing, he knoweth nothing yet as he ought to know.

So, maybe I don't know what I need to know about suicidal death… Maybe I am wrong about this evil spirit and if so you win… I am writing this book full of God's word in hope you who have been thinking about suicidal death may read a scripture you never read and look at it as being a sin, not a penalty for taking your own life. It's not that I don't understand why one may want to take their life… What I am saying is that we gain nothing by taking our own life for whatsoever reason. I truly hope there is a word in this book or a scripture from God's word that may give you a reason for living with hope. I pray that it will help you to encourage yourself or even reach out for help. The reason for all of the scripture references is that I am hoping you see that someone long before our times had some of the same situations or little different. But, the same struggle shows you how over come.

1 Corinthians 8:2

² And if any man think that he knoweth any thing, he knoweth nothing
yet as he ought to know.

Section Two

Continually showing my love, sympathy and prayer because of my experience, beliefs and the little I know of God, that we will not destroy thyself by committing suicide. Yes, there may be six good reasons why one may want to commit suicidal death. They are tired of struggling because of low self-esteem, misfortune and from being bullied because of failure and bitterness. The reason I can relate to these things is because from the age of sixteen I too struggled with some of the same situations. With God's help I am trying to encourage you that suicidal death is not the way out. So, if you feel life has shown you no favor on this side, then who told you that death will show you favor on the other side? I am saying that we know what trouble we are facing on this side but we may be surprised what we will face on the other side. So, I hope something that you read in this book may encourage you to ride out your trouble and struggles on this side and not commit suicidal death. Then if you had to wait it out on the other side, and the expectant then becomes the unexpected think about it.

1 John 3:15

> ¹⁵ Whosoever hateth his brother is a murderer: and ye know that no murderer hath eternal life abiding in him.

If you feel there are a few reasons to commit suicidal death, there may be a few reasons you may "not" want too.

1. We do not know what's after death
2. It could be considered murder
3. Life we know about, death is something we wonder about…

Ride It Out On This Side Or Wait It Out On The Other Side

Whether we believe it or not, we all must come face to face with death one day.

But, let it be God's choice. I believe there is a price we pay for every choice we make, whether it is good or bad. Life is given by God, just as death is promise by God.

Hebrews 9:27

²⁷ And as it is appointed unto men once to die, but after this the judgment:

Romans 14:10

¹⁰ But why dost thou judge thy brother? or why dost thou set at nought thy brother? for we shall all stand before the judgment seat of Christ.

2 Corinthians 5:10

¹⁰ For we must all appear before the judgment seat of Christ; that every one may receive the things done in his body, according to that he hath done, whether it be good or bad.

Now with that being said, if these scriptures are true and if suicidal death is murder, and if it's a crime against God's Law then that should give us a lot to think upon before doing it. I used the term "if" because it is said to be a subrogate conjunction; it deepens on something else. So if one commits suicidal death it is their choice. But, if it is considered murder in God's eyes then it becomes God's choice to choose the result.

Revelation 21:8

⁸ But the fearful, and unbelieving, and the abominable, and murderers, and whoremongers, and sorcerers, and idolaters, and all liars, shall have their part in the lake which burneth with fire and brimstone: which is the second death.

Let's say that this scripture is true… I say this because I believe in God and His words. Would it be safe to say you know or believe suicidal death is okay with God? Or, is it a cop out? But, I will say to you that it could be a force by an unknown spirit that you may not beware off. This spirit can enter one like death with no smell, taste or feeling when it enters.

Luke 22:3

³ Then entered Satan into Judas surnamed Iscariot, being of the number of the twelve.

Matthew 27:5

⁵ And he cast down the pieces of silver in the temple, and departed, and went and hanged himself.

Let us look at Paul, one who was saved & converted by God.

Romans 7:15-20

¹⁵ For that which I do I allow not: for what I would, that do I not; but what I hate, that do I.
¹⁶ If then I do that which I would not, I consent unto the law that it is good.
¹⁷ Now then it is no more I that do it, but sin that dwelleth in me.
¹⁸ For I know that in me (that is, in my flesh,) dwelleth no good thing: for to will is

present with me; but how to perform that which is good I find not.
¹⁹ For the good that I would I do not: but the evil which I would not, that I do.
²⁰ Now if I do that I would not, it is no more I that do it, but sin that dwelleth in me.

My friends this is that evil spirit that enters a man which had been converted by God. With God we can know this evil spirit. I want you to understand this spirit is real... So suicidal death can be foes from within... But, I will say this: whether it's suicidal or natural death, we will have to wait for the result...

Revelation 6:9-10

⁹ And when he had opened the fifth seal, I saw under the altar the souls of them that were slain for the word of God, and for the testimony which they held:
¹⁰ And they cried with a loud voice, saying, How long, O Lord, holy and true, dost thou not judge and avenge our blood on them that dwell on the earth?

I used the word "if" because I believe every scripture in God's word is true. There are those who do not believe and there are those who are unsure. Either way, we'll have to wait and see the facts. So I say, ride it out on this side or wait it out on the other side.

TO THOSE WHO COMMIT SUICIDAL DEATH, BECAUSE OF BEING BULLIED

I know we all think different and react to situations differently, whether it's being bullied or struggling with life as whole. Maybe the same can be said about being bullied. Their struggle in life can cause them to see those same struggles within you. He or she knowing that you have low-self-esteem, low self-conscious, and insecure feelings, will use it against you because they have been watching you way before they approached you. Most bullies grow up with low self-esteem and may have grown up feeling isolated. They see pain in you and make you a target...

I say this to you from the experience of growing up in Mississippi as a very poor black man... But, I learned if you show no sign of weakness then you can overcome the bully. Fear is one of the worst nightmares a person can have. But, due to the laws having being put in place my advice to you is this. If you're being bulled in school go to your principal or teacher. Also, go to your parents and siblings at home. If you're being bullied while around other people, scream out loud and never be alone again. Don't fear their threats. If they threaten to kill your family reach out to someone. Someone bullied may have mental problems... Notice their actions when he or she is approached. Most bullies are looking for attention because they grow up with low-self-esteem or without friends and want someone to love them. So they prey on and target you. Then they begin to terrorize you because they see some of same weaknesses in you as they see in themselves. I have learned that most bullies act out when others are around them. They try to impress them because he or she is looking for love or a friend. I have also learned that most bullies are cowards themselves. It seems that bullies have become a major problem in the schools. The law and those in charge of the schools need to come together to find ways to deal with situations involving them. Don't wait until another twelve year old commits suicide.

To those of you thinking about committing suicidal death because someone has wrongly labeled or doesn't love you, know that you have allowed low-esteem to set in. This is because the one you love has not shown you love. That makes you want to commit suicidal death. One must first love God and themselves. Always love yourself regardless of your outlook on life and regardless of what you are going through. Love yourself regardless of who doesn't love you or does not want to be friends with you. As long as you are loved by God and your family you know that you are being loved by someone. When we see ourselves as an outcast, we fail to be what God and our parents hoped for us to be. When we thirst for something it doesn't mean we need it. It's something we may just want... Things we want and don't have can make us feel like a failure. It's not that we are failures; it's just that some things did not work out as we had planned at the time. But, if we commit suicidal death we will never know how many positive opportunities we may have missed out on. Suicidal death eliminated all possibilities of all we could be and hope to be... If you allow the bully to push you into suicidal death, you never know whether he or she were who they seemed to be because you gave in to their pressure.

Ride It Out On This Side Or Wait It Out On The Other Side

Our first mistake is when we accept what they say. Then we feel intimidated by their words because of our lack of confidence within ourselves. Then low self-esteem sets in our minds and the mind keeps reminding us of what they said, as we struggle with not knowing who we are. Second, don't be a people pleaser. Love yourself regardless of your struggle, disappointment, misfortune or failure. Not all of us please people with our looks. Nor were we all born to be rich or poor. You are not the only one in this world that is unhappy with life's struggle. But, do we know what death has to offer will make us more happy? Believe me, I know struggle in the form of unhappiness, misfortune, disappointment, aggravation, depression, and failure. From the age of sixteen and even to this day I am dealing with some of the same issues. I was labeled as a "nigger". I did not know what a "nigger" was except for a black man... I live with it... My first name was "nigger" and my last name was boy from the mouths of most white people. I had low self-esteem, but never felt less than a man. My motivation was when I would become grown I would overcome being a poor man... So don't let being labeled or name calling make you feel less than a man or woman.

Your struggles in life may cause you to want to commit suicidal death. I have learned all tricks that the enemy uses to get to our minds as we go through life. So the way we think can cause sorrow or put us in a comfort or danger zone. The reason why I say this is found in this scripture:

Proverbs 23:7

⁷ For as he thinketh in his heart, so is he: Eat and drink, saith he to thee; but his heart is not with thee.

The enemy knows how we act and speak according to the way we feel about different situations...

1 Peter 5:8

⁸ Be sober, be vigilant; because your adversary the devil, as a roaring lion, walketh about, seeking whom he may devour:

My friend's, this scripture is to let you know that when you think about suicidal death you may have a demonic influence over your life. Then, maybe you understand this scripture when we find ourselves struggling within:

Ephesians 6:12

¹² For we wrestle not against flesh and blood, but against principalities, against powers, against the rulers of the darkness of this world, against spiritual wickedness in high places

Know this as well my friends. Suicidal death can be physical, mental, or spiritual.

Vester Dock

Galatians 5:17

17 For the flesh lusteth against the Spirit, and the Spirit against the flesh: and these are contrary the one to the other: so that ye cannot do the things that ye would.

Section Three

I'm hoping as you go to through this chapter that you will take advice from this book and second guess your decision on committing suicidal death. If you are feeling that you are at your wits end. Take Solomon at his words:

Proverbs 3:5-6

[5] Trust in the Lord with all thine heart; and lean not unto thine own understanding.
[6] In all thy ways acknowledge him, and he shall direct thy paths.

Believe me, there is a price to pay for every choice we make; whether it's good or bad. All I am saying is let death be God's choice. Believe me or not, the results will be God's choice. We knoweth what we struggle with on this side, but if there is another side after death and the grave we may be surprised with what awaits us on the other side. The expected could be the unexpected... My friends, this is the devil known as Satan. He is the very evil spirit the bible speaks of.

He is very, very real. I want us to be able to recognize this spirit. He is called the Tempter; the wicked one and the Prince of the air. He is the ruler of this world who often disguises himself as a serpent. I remind you it possess us when we listen to the wrong voice. This is when we think of experiencing a suicidal death.

2 Corinthians 11:14-15

[14] And no marvel; for Satan himself is transformed into an angel of light.
[15] Therefore it is no great thing if his ministers also be transformed as the ministers of righteousness; whose end shall be according to their works.

Ride It Out On This Side Or Wait It Out On The Other Side

As I come to the close of this book. I say as Paul:

1 Corinthians 9:19-20

¹⁹ For though I be free from all men, yet have I made myself servant unto all, that I might gain the more.
²⁰ And unto the Jews I became as a Jew, that I might gain the Jews; to them that are under the law, as under the law, that I might gain them that are under the law;

1 Corinthians 9:22

²² To the weak became I as weak, that I might gain the weak: I am made all things to all men, that I might by all means save some.

I believe if I can reach one with the words in this book and that one teach one to love one, and that one loved one, then I believe it would be less lost ones. I used the scripture because I believe:

2 Timothy 3:16

[16] All scripture is given by inspiration of God, and is profitable for doctrine, for reproof, for correction, for instruction in righteousness:

My friend's with that being said let us turn to two other books that we know was written by man.

1. Webster Dictionary
2. Encyclopedia

If these two books have the correct definition to every word written in them then I will say they were given inspiration by God. God is infinite while man is finite. Man is subject to making mistakes and them being proved. God's word never has been proved wrong. God has had the first say over our lives and God will have last say after our death. If you never thought about it, it's the same God that gave life and he also created death. God also has given the devil the power he has and permits him to attack and control him. He does everything else on earth and heaven. Facts are facts... We can believe it, deny it, hate it, neglect it, resist it, or oppose it but we cannot change or erase it. So regardless of how we die may God have mercy on our souls.

When we say may God have mercy on our soul's, by us not believing something does not make it wrong or cause us to believe something does not say it's always right. Am I right in all I believe? "**NO!**" But I do believe all these things we want and have on this side, the same as life, are temporary. I believe the scripture:

2 Corinthians 4:18

¹⁸ While we look not at the things which are seen, but at the things which are not seen: for the things which are seen are temporal; but the things which are not seen are eternal.

Let's say death is a mystery because I believe this scripture also:

1 Corinthians 8:2

² And if any man think that he knoweth any thing, he knoweth nothing yet as he ought to know.

Do I know what happens to you for committing suicidal death? No... Do I know what's going to happen to me when I die? No... My hope and belief is to live eternal with the Lord somewhere. Neither my life nor my destiny is in my control. I believe God is in full control and He has the final say... So if your dilemma or struggle in life has pushed you to the point of thinking suicidal death, I pray you seek help and ask yourself these questions: If I commit suicidal death, is it wrong? If God doesn't approve it and it's a sin, is there is a penalty? If there is a hell, will I go there?

If you do not have the answer to any of these questions then my sincere hope and prayer is that you say, "I won't do it." Whatever troubles you have in life, ride it out on this side with hope or wait it out on the other side. We do not know the outcome.

Parent's help your children from being bullied into suicidal death. Watch your children more closely than usual. Parents our kids are challenged by things that they are facing today... Parenting is more than giving life... Watch our children's motion, change of attitude, and when they start to stay alone in their room more & more. They may be seeking more attention or more love. You can help by having a family talk once a week and let them express themselves in the way they know how; even if you think it's disrespectful. Most of you parents think it is wrong to interfere in their privacy. As parents we must always ask ourselves "What I am not doing?" and stop accepting what we think is alright. You may be able to save your child from this bully. When your child is being bullied you may be the first to know. You take it to the school and the law. If they do not take care the situation, as a parent talk to the bully. Most bullies are cowards and they target and terrorize your child to gain a false sense of power.

Yes we may have laws against bullies but if these laws are not in the schools then you must protect your child. What good are they after your child is dead? Stop talking about you don't have the money to pay the cops to be stationed in the schools. If bullying is causing suicidal death, protect our kid's lives in our schools by showing us that our tax dollar is being well spent. Parents lets put more quality time in with our children. Listen to what your child has to say. It may prevent an accident before it happens because pastors, preachers and police commit suicidal death too. It does not mean the punishment for suicidal death changes. The evil spirit can pervade believers as none believers. Why, because he or she is listening to the wrong voice…

Mark 13:22

²² For false Christs and false prophets shall rise, and shall shew signs and wonders, to seduce, if it were possible, even the elect.

Not that I know, so maybe some these pastors and preachers are false that commit suicidal death. We may not know who is who but this evil spirit knoweth...

1 Peter 5:8

8 Be sober, be vigilant; because your adversary the devil, as a roaring lion, walketh about, seeking whom he may devour:

I end it this way, because I am writing for non believers as well as believers. In this book, the Holy Bible knoweth there are some who don't know what to believe. Satan influences and engages in worldly affairs. This is clearly revealed as his various titles reflect his control of the world system as the ruler of this world.

John 12:31

31 Now is the judgment of this world: now shall the **prince of this world** be cast out.

2 Corinthians 4:4

4 In whom **the god of this world** hath blinded the minds of them which believe not, lest the light of the glorious gospel of Christ, who is the image of God, should shine unto them.

Ephesians 2:2

2 Wherein in time past ye walked according to the course of this world, according to **the prince of the power of the air**, the spirit that now worketh in the children of disobedience:

1 John 5:19

19 And we know that we are of God, and **the whole world lieth in wickedness.**

Matthew 12:24

24 But when the Pharisees heard it, they said, This fellow doth not cast out devils, but by **Beelzebub the prince of the devils.**

I pray & hope this book will save someone from suicidal death. I feel your pain.

This evil spirit I talk about in this book is something that I don't hear too many television ministries or pastors talking about from the pulpit today, as if he doesn't exist... I'll put it this way; this evil spirit is somewhat like a bully. Not that he knoweth what we are thinking, but most of us show our thinking by our actions. Bullies and this evil spirit both notice our actions. Our actions can expose our true nature or are true character from deep within.

Our weaknesses, motives, ambition, desires and thinking are all exposed... this how I believe we expose ourselves to the bully and the evil spirit. The devil is the one who I believe controls this evil spirit. The devil is called an impersonator and we do not need to have a degree to know an impersonator. We don't even have to be a believer in God, nor His word, to know an impersonator. Just look at leadership in the world today. Many have proved themselves to be an impersonator. Whether it is a preacher, pastor, government official, law enforcement as well as a bully... I base this on experience and this scripture:

Ride It Out On This Side Or Wait It Out On The Other Side

2 Corinthians 11:13-15

¹³ For such are false apostles, deceitful workers, transforming themselves into the apostles of Christ.
¹⁴ And no marvel; for Satan himself is transformed into an angel of light.
¹⁵ Therefore it is no great thing if his ministers also be transformed as the ministers of righteousness; whose end shall be according to their works.

You who are thinking of committing suicidal death ask yourself, "Is committing suicide my work? If so, what will my end be?" I may be wrong but I believe bullying and suicidal death is enforced by this impersonator. I do believe he can attack our mind and influence us into making wrong decisions. An unstable mind can be easy persuaded, when it shows signs of weakness.

James 1:8

⁸ A double minded man is unstable in all his ways.

A double minded man is unstable in all his ways. Remember that I said neither this evil spirit nor the bully knows what you are thinking but I believe both watch your actions. The frauds actions speak louder than words showing low self-esteem, lack of confidence within you shows signs of weakness. This is how the bully puts fear within you and this influences us to speak doubt within ourselves. Ultimately our actions are revealed to the impersonator, Satan.

1 Peter 5:8

⁸ Be sober, be vigilant; because your adversary the devil, as a roaring lion, walketh about, seeking whom he may devour:

My friends this is a short book and I hope all who are thinking about committing suicidal death as a way out of your situation or dilemma truly stop and reflect. Recognize the test of the bully before you take your own life. Pick up this book and seek help. You may ask "Vester Dock can you help us?" Neither I nor you will know unless we give it a try. I am not saying I can give you what you need, but if you are willing take this book and read it than I am willing to give it my shot. I believe if we all take Solomon at his words rather than commit suicidal death it will give you another chance to ride it out on this side rather than wait it out on the other side.

Proverbs 3:5-6

[5] Trust in the Lord with all thine heart; and lean not unto thine own understanding.
[6] In all thy ways acknowledge him, and he shall direct thy paths.

In my closing, we may not believe in God or His words, nor believe in Heaven or Hell or believe in life after death. One thing we know is the facts of life and death. If we become impatient on this side because we're feeling life has failed us in so many ways... When all the twists and turns in life begin to make us feel helpless, hopeless, and bitter and begin to make us feel less fortune than others we need to encourage ourselves and seek help if necessary. But ask yourselves what you can gain by suicidal death. Does death offer more than life?

I say I don't know but I will say this. Death is a one way ticket with no return. Whatever causes us to want to commit suicidal death when being attacked by a bully. Remember, if you do commit suicidal death... the bully wins and you lose. Challenge your bully; meaning always look them in the eyes and never looking down! If sitting down, stand to your feet and don't talk to them because your voice may show signs of weakness. Remember, the bully as well the impersonator of this evil spirit watch your actions… If we become impatient on this side with life, death will cause you to become patient on the other side.

Ride It Out On This Side Or Wait It Out On The Other Side

I will admit that I am not one hundred percent sure about the other side but I am one hundred percent about God: the Father, the Son, and Holy Spirit. But, I am not ninety percent wrong about what I have written in this book. Fact is, some of it is from experience along with what I believe in God's word.

Resources

**For anyone in suicidal crisis
or emotional distress.**
National Suicide Prevention Lifeline
Call 1-800-273-8255
Available 24 hours everyday
The Lifeline provides 24/7, free and confidential
support for people in distress.
http://www.suicide.org/suicide-hotlines.html

Bullying

https://www.stopbullying.gov/

What Is Bullying

Bullying is unwanted, aggressive behavior among school aged children that involves a real or perceived power imbalance. The behavior is repeated, or has the potential to be repeated, over time. Both kids who are bullied and who bully others may have serious, lasting problems.

In order to be considered bullying, the behavior must be aggressive and include:
- **An Imbalance of Power:** Kids who bully use their power—such as physical strength, access to embarrassing information, or popularity—to control or harm others. Power imbalances can change over time and in different situations, even if they involve the same people.
- **Repetition:** Bullying behaviors happen more than once or have the potential to happen more than once.

Bullying includes actions such as making threats, spreading rumors, attacking someone physically or verbally, and excluding someone from a group on purpose.

Types of Bullying

There are three types of bullying:
- **Verbal bullying** is saying or writing mean things. Verbal bullying includes:
    - Teasing
    - Name-calling
    - Inappropriate sexual comments
    - Taunting
    - Threatening to cause harm
- **Social bullying,** sometimes referred to as relational bullying, involves hurting someone's reputation or relationships. Social bullying includes:
    - Leaving someone out on purpose
    - Telling other children not to be friends with someone
    - Spreading rumors about someone
    - Embarrassing someone in public
- **Physical bullying** involves hurting a person's body or possessions. Physical bullying includes:
    - Hitting/kicking/pinching
    - Spitting
    - Tripping/pushing
    - Taking or breaking someone's things
    - Making mean or rude hand gestures

Where and When Bullying Happens

Bullying can occur during or after school hours. While most reported bullying happens in the school building, a significant percentage also happens in places like on the playground or the bus. It can also happen travelling to or from school, in the youth's neighborhood, or on the Internet.

Prevention

Teach kids how to identify bullying and how to stand up to it safely.

Be aware of what your kids are doing online.

What Is Cyberbullying

Cyberbullying is bullying that takes place over digital devices like cell phones, computers, and tablets. Cyberbullying can occur through SMS, Text, and apps, or online in social media, forums, or gaming where people can view, participate in, or share content. Cyberbullying includes sending, posting, or sharing negative, harmful, false, or mean content about someone else. It can include sharing personal or private information about someone else causing embarrassment or humiliation. Some cyberbullying crosses the line into unlawful or criminal behavior.

The most common places where cyberbullying occurs are:
- Social Media, such as Facebook, Instagram, Snapchat, and Twitter
- SMS (Short Message Service) also known as Text Message sent through devices
- Instant Message (via devices, email provider services, apps, and social media messaging features)
- Email

Special Concerns

With the prevalence of social media and digital forums, comments, photos, posts, and content shared by individuals can often be viewed by strangers as well as acquaintances. The content an individual shares online – both their personal content as well as any negative, mean, or hurtful content – creates a kind of permanent public record of their views, activities, and behavior. This public record can be thought of as an online reputation, which may be accessible to schools, employers, colleges, clubs, and others who may be researching an individual now or in the future. Cyberbullying can harm the online reputations of everyone involved – not just the person being bullied, but those doing the bullying or participating in it. Cyberbullying has unique concerns in that it can be:

Persistent – Digital devices offer an ability to immediately and continuously communicate 24 hours a day, so it can be difficult for children experiencing cyberbullying to find relief.

Permanent – Most information communicated electronically is permanent and public, if not reported and removed. A negative online reputation, including for those who bully, can impact college admissions, employment, and other areas of life.

Hard to Notice – Because teachers and parents may not overhear or see cyberbullying taking place, it is harder to recognize.

Laws and Sanctions

While all states have criminal laws that apply to bullying, not all have special statutes that apply to cyberbullying or bullying that takes place outside of school. Schools may take action either as required by law, or with local or school policies that allow them to discipline or take other action. Some states also have provisions to address bullying if it affects school performance. You can learn about the laws and policies in each state, including if they cover cyberbullying.

GET HELP NOW!

If you have done everything you can to resolve the situation and nothing has worked, or someone is in immediate danger, there are ways to get help.

- If there has been a crime or someone is at immediate risk of harm. **Call 911.**

- If someone is feeling hopeless, helpless, thinking of suicide. Contact the National Suicide Prevention Lifeline online at http://www.suicide.org/suicidehotlines.html or at **1-800-273-TALK (8255)**.
  The toll-free call goes to the nearest crisis center in our national network. These centers provide 24-hour crisis counseling and mental health referrals.

- If someone is being bullied in school.
    Contact the:
    1. Teacher
    2. School counselor
    3. School principal
    4. School superintendent
    5. State Department of Education

Veterans

Crisis Line - **Call 1-800-273-8255** and Press 1

For veterans, crises can be heightened by their experiences during military service. If you're a veteran or service member and in crisis, these resources can help.

https://www.veteranscrisisline.net/

The Veterans Crisis Line connects Veterans in crisis and their families and friends with qualified, caring Department of Veterans Affairs responders through a confidential toll-free hotline, online chat, or text.

Veterans and their loved ones can call 1-800-273-8255 and Press 1, chat online, or send a text message to 838255 to receive confidential support 24 hours a day, 7 days a week, 365 days a year. Support for deaf and hard of hearing individuals is available.

Notes & Reflections

A place to write down your thoughts and feelings and reflect on life.

Notes & Reflections

Day:_____ Date:_____ Time:_____

Notes & Reflections

Day:_____ Date:_____ Time:_____

Notes& Reflections

Day:_____ Date:_____ Time:_____

_____
_____
_____
_____
_____
_____
_____
_____
_____
_____
_____
_____
_____
_____
_____
_____
_____
_____
_____
_____
_____

Notes& Reflections

Day:_____ Date:_____ Time:_____

_____
_____
_____
_____
_____
_____
_____
_____
_____
_____
_____
_____
_____
_____
_____
_____
_____
_____
_____
_____
_____
_____

Notes& Reflections

Day:_____ Date:_____ Time:_____

Notes& Reflections

Day:_____ Date:_____ Time:_____

Notes& Reflections

Day:_____ Date:_____ Time:_____

_____
_____
_____
_____
_____
_____
_____
_____
_____
_____
_____
_____
_____
_____
_____
_____
_____
_____
_____
_____
_____
_____
_____
_____
_____

Notes& Reflections

Day:_____ Date:_____ Time:_____

Notes& Reflections

Day:_____ Date:_____ Time:_____

Notes & Reflections

Day:_____ Date:_____ Time:_____

Notes& Reflections

Day:_____ Date:_____ Time:_____

Notes& Reflections

Day:_____ Date:_____ Time:_____

_____
_____
_____
_____
_____
_____
_____
_____
_____
_____
_____
_____
_____
_____
_____
_____
_____
_____
_____
_____
_____
_____
_____
_____

Notes& Reflections

Day:_____ Date:_____ Time:_____

_____
_____
_____
_____
_____
_____
_____
_____
_____
_____
_____
_____
_____
_____
_____
_____
_____
_____
_____
_____
_____
_____

Notes& Reflections

Day:_____ Date:_____ Time:_____

Notes& Reflections

Day:_____ Date:_____ Time:_____

Notes & Reflections

*Day:*_____ *Date:*_____ *Time:*_____

Notes & Reflections

Day:_____ Date:_____ Time:_____

_____

_____

_____

_____

_____

_____

_____

_____

_____

_____

_____

_____

_____

_____

_____

_____

_____

_____

_____

_____

_____

Notes& Reflections

*Day:*_____ *Date:*_____ *Time:*_____

Notes& Reflections

Day:_____ Date:_____ Time:_____

Notes & Reflections

Day:_____ Date:_____ Time:_____

_____
_____
_____
_____
_____
_____
_____
_____
_____
_____
_____
_____
_____
_____
_____
_____
_____
_____
_____
_____
_____
_____
_____
_____

Notes& Reflections

Day:_____ Date:_____ Time:_____

Notes & Reflections

Day:_____ Date:_____ Time:_____

_____

_____

_____

_____

_____

_____

_____

_____

_____

_____

_____

_____

_____

_____

_____

_____

_____

_____

_____

_____

_____

_____

Notes& Reflections

Day:_____ Date:_____ Time:_____

_____
_____
_____
_____
_____
_____
_____
_____
_____
_____
_____
_____
_____
_____
_____
_____
_____
_____
_____
_____
_____
_____
_____

Notes& Reflections

Day:_____ Date:_____ Time:_____

Notes & Reflections

Day:_____ Date:_____ Time:_____

_____
_____
_____
_____
_____
_____
_____
_____
_____
_____
_____
_____
_____
_____
_____
_____
_____
_____
_____
_____
_____
_____
_____
_____

Notes& Reflections

Day:_____ Date:_____ Time:_____

Notes& Reflections

Day:_____ Date:_____ Time:_____

_____
_____
_____
_____
_____
_____
_____
_____
_____
_____
_____
_____
_____
_____
_____
_____
_____
_____
_____
_____
_____
_____

Notes& Reflections

Day:_____ Date:_____ Time:_____

_____
_____
_____
_____
_____
_____
_____
_____
_____
_____
_____
_____
_____
_____
_____
_____
_____
_____
_____
_____
_____
_____

Notes& Reflections

Day:_____ Date:_____ Time:_____

_____
_____
_____
_____
_____
_____
_____
_____
_____
_____
_____
_____
_____
_____
_____
_____
_____
_____
_____
_____
_____
_____

Notes& Reflections

*Day:*_____ *Date:*_____ *Time:*_____

Notes& Reflections

Day:_____ Date:_____ Time:_____

_____
_____
_____
_____
_____
_____
_____
_____
_____
_____
_____
_____
_____
_____
_____
_____
_____
_____
_____
_____
_____

Notes& Reflections

Day:_____ Date:_____ Time:_____

Notes & Reflections

Day:_____ Date:_____ Time:_____

_____
_____
_____
_____
_____
_____
_____
_____
_____
_____
_____
_____
_____
_____
_____
_____
_____
_____
_____
_____
_____
_____

Notes& Reflections

*Day:*_____ *Date:*_____ *Time:*_____

Notes& Reflections

Day:_____ Date:_____ Time:_____

Notes& Reflections

Day:_____ Date:_____ Time:_____

_____
_____
_____
_____
_____
_____
_____
_____
_____
_____
_____
_____
_____
_____
_____
_____
_____
_____
_____
_____
_____
_____

Notes& Reflections

Day:_____ Date:_____ Time:_____

_____

_____

_____

_____

_____

_____

_____

_____

_____

_____

_____

_____

_____

_____

_____

_____

_____

_____

_____

_____

_____

Notes& Reflections

Day:_____ Date:_____ Time:_____

_____
_____
_____
_____
_____
_____
_____
_____
_____
_____
_____
_____
_____
_____
_____
_____
_____
_____
_____
_____
_____
_____

Notes & Reflections

Day:_____ Date:_____ Time:_____

_____

_____

_____

_____

_____

_____

_____

_____

_____

_____

_____

_____

_____

_____

_____

_____

_____

_____

_____

_____

_____

_____

Notes& Reflections

Day:_____ Date:_____ Time:_____

Notes& Reflections

Day:_____ Date:_____ Time:_____

Notes& Reflections

Day:_____ Date:_____ Time:_____

Notes& Reflections

Day:_____ Date:_____ Time:_____

_____
_____
_____
_____
_____
_____
_____
_____
_____
_____
_____
_____
_____
_____
_____
_____
_____
_____
_____
_____
_____
_____

Notes & Reflections

Day:_____ Date:_____ Time:_____

_____
_____
_____
_____
_____
_____
_____
_____
_____
_____
_____
_____
_____
_____
_____
_____
_____
_____
_____
_____
_____
_____
_____

Notes& Reflections

Day:_____ Date:_____ Time:_____

Notes & Reflections

Day:_____ Date:_____ Time:_____

Notes& Reflections

Day:_____ Date:_____ Time:_____

Notes& Reflections

Day:_____ Date:_____ Time:_____

Notes& Reflections

Day:_____ Date:_____ Time:_____

Notes& Reflections

Day:_____ Date:_____ Time:_____

Notes& Reflections

Day:_____ Date:_____ Time:_____

Notes& Reflections

Day:_____ Date:_____ Time:_____

Notes& Reflections

*Day:*_____ *Date:*_____ *Time:*_____

Notes& Reflections

Day:_____ Date:_____ Time:_____

Notes& Reflections

Day:_____ Date:_____ Time:_____

Notes & Reflections

Day:_____ Date:_____ Time:_____

Notes& Reflections

Day:_____ Date:_____ Time:_____

Notes& Reflections

Day:_____ Date:_____ Time:_____

Notes& Reflections

Day:_____ Date:_____ Time:_____

Notes & Reflections

Day:_____ Date:_____ Time:_____

About the Author

Vester Dock

I am from Mississippi. At the age of 16, I found myself on my own after my mother's death with no job, just working on a farm. There was one family that I will never forget. Their last name was Baskins; they were there for me when my mother passed away.

I married at the age of 20 and after three years of marriage; I was forced to move. What was so amazing to Gail (my great niece) is that I left Mississippi with three shirts, a pair of pants, and the shoes on my feet, oh and I only had five dollars in my pocket. I traveled to California and even played some semi-professional baseball but I never forgot about my family.

Now as a young man I didn't always believe in God but I always knew that there is a God. Now I know that it was God that made it possible to re-unite me with my family and bring them to New Jersey. There were 15 of us living in a five room apartment in 1965. God brought us through and has kept us as a family every since. Currently I am an ordained Minister. I have been preaching since 1983.

Contact Vester Dock

e-mail: vdock1940@gmail.com
or jayshoya9899@gmail.com

www.ingramcontent.com/pod-product-compliance
Lightning Source LLC
Chambersburg PA
CBHW071708040426
42446CB00011B/1966